Let's Go to the
Zoo

By Cate Foley

Welcome
Books

SCHOLASTIC INC.

New York Toronto London Auckland Sydney
Mexico City New Delhi Hong Kong Buenos Aires

Photo Credits: Cover and all photos by Maura Boruchow

Contributing Editors: Jeri Cipriano, Jennifer Silate
Book Design: Victoria Johnson

ISBN 0-516-24505-8

12 11 10   13 14/0

Printed in China.   62

First Scholastic printing, September 2002

Contents

We are going to
the zoo today.

5

There are many animals in the zoo.

First, I want to see the bears.

I like **polar bears.**

I like to watch them swim.

Today, they just want to rest.

9

We also see ducks.

They are very pretty!

Next, we visit the **seals.**

They are sitting on the rocks.

The **zookeeper** brings food.

It is time for the seals to eat.

The zookeeper throws
fish to them.

15

I am hungry, too.

I will eat a **pretzel.**

It is getting late.

We see the monkeys before we leave.

Which animal do you like best?

21

New Words

polar bears (**poh**-luhr **bairz**) large white bears of the arctic region

pretzel (**preht**-suhl) a kind of bread in the shape of a knot

seals (**seelz**) sea mammals with large flippers

zookeeper (**zoo**-kee-puhr) a person who cares for animals in a zoo

To Find Out More

Books
Animals in the Zoo
by Allan Fowler
Children's Press

Jungle Jack Hanna's What Zoo Keepers Do
by Jack Hanna
Scholastic Inc.

Web Site
San Diego Zoo
http://www.sandiegozoo.org
You can visit many areas of this Web site and learn about different animals.

Index

About the Author

Cate Foley writes and edits books for children. She lives in New Jersey with her husband and son.

Reading Consultants

Kris Flynn, Coordinator, Small School District Literacy, The San Diego County Office of Education

Shelly Forys, Certified Reading Recovery Specialist, W.J. Zahnow Elementary School, Waterloo, IL

Sue McAdams, Certified Reading Recovery Specialist and Literary Consultant, Dallas, TX